OUT FROM CALABOOSE

Nirala Series
OUT FROM CALABOOSE

Karen Corinne Herceg graduated from Columbia University with a B.A. in Literature/Writing. Her first volume of poetry is *Inner Sanctions*. *Out From Calaboose* is her second volume.

A recipient of New York State grants, Karen has read at various venues, universities and libraries on programs featuring such renowned poets as Pulitzer Prize winner John Ashbery and has studied and featured with poets David Ignatow and Pulitzer Prize winner Philip Schultz. She publishes poetry, prose, and essays.

Karen is a member of Poets & Writers, the Academy of American Poets, PEN America, The Poetry Society of America and C.A.P.S. and is a featured poet on the New York poetry scene. Her website is www.karencorinneherceg.com and you can also follow her on Facebook and Twitter @ #karen_herceg. She resides in the Hudson Valley, New York.

The role of the poet is to stay abnormal.

Brenda Hillman

Praise for
Karen Corinne Herceg

Clutching her vision firmly in hand, Karen Corinne Herceg paints her inner world in such a vivid fashion that I was compelled to submerge myself in Out From Calaboose *completely, and then not surface at all until I put down the last poem. What I wove through during the course of that reading was a feast: imagery fine enough that it startled; rhythms that wove from poem to poem, joining all their music together; and language so sleek that not one word had been left standing if it ought not to be. In this collection, Herceg brings us her life and all its many emotional truths, some ugly, some beautiful, but all revealed with restraint--so that by book's end, we are left in wonder.*

–**Linda Gray Sexton**, author of *Searching for Mercy Street: My Journey Back To My Mother, Anne Sexton* and *Half In Love: Surviving The Legacy Of Suicide*

Herceg is a grand 'maker' in our Eastern tradition, an emergence of a fresh American voice that pulls out of her past a dark abyss of time, 'herding children, objects and desires' and brings along her story with a 'feline intensity,' very much like her cats, never looking hurt, 'just indignant.' Here are poems racing against the chill of time and treacherous tides that have washed away years of a young woman who stands now at the threshold of life with 'her grocery bags' and sings songs of the new, her new hope in 'greens and fruits' tethered to 'a grassy firmament,' birthing through 'a placenta of debts', cutting umbilical cords, dragging herself through the mire of inherited sins in a 'maternal bloodbath,' a place where her parents rest in sullen 'drawers of steel.' This is a remarkable work, a Virginia Woolf moment stretched into a book of poems, or a Whitman rumination that refuses to come to an end, enamored as it is by life's ongoing rush. Out from Calaboose *affirms Herceg's faith in a poet's visionary status as she imagines her hand reaching toward, snapping through 'embryonic clay' and sculpting lives that could become whole...*

–**Yuyutsu Sharma**, Himalayan Poet & author of *Quaking Cantos: Nepal Earthquake Poems* and *A Blizzard in my Bones: New York Poems*

Often it is a pronounced sense of wonder that makes poets like Karen Corinne Herceg. In her volume, Out From Calaboose, she is Alice in her Wonderland, a curious child asking Why? Why? Why? Why are "our impatient lives [spent] in fluorescent lit aisles"? Why can a mother only offer "left over hippie love before the dusk of empty bottles"? Why is it that "time chimes clocks as if it were a gift"? And why do we [keep] "kicking [ourselves] back onto the cross, always just shy of resurrection"? When a child asks Why, she expects a truthful answer. So does Herceg. She wants to get to the bottom of just why we break out of our birth shells so passionately, with biting egg teeth, only to construct invisible shields, brick and mortar walls and personal calabooses that separate us from each other. What drives us? What forces impose themselves on us? The poems in Out From Calaboose compile a quest for truthful answers, one of which Herceg instinctively knows when she quotes Carl Sagan at the beginning of her poem "Alternatives" – "for small creatures such as we the vastness is bearable only through love."
–Janet Hamill, Poet, Performance Artist

In her powerful new volume, Out from Calaboose, Karen Herceg clearly demonstrates the loneliness and wonder of a "world scaled for living"(from "Tableau"). Herceg's is a world fueled by travel, whether it is global wanderings or the travelings of a troubled spirit seeking rest or resolution: "Will anything stave off this thing/called salvation--/how if we pine and ponder enough/ somehow we will deserve explanations" (from "After Me, The Poem"). Her verse can often be troubling, as when she describes the transparent boundaries separating creatures from nature (the immolation of birds as they hit pane glass, a sacrifice to hubris); culture from culture; people from each other; and humans from nature: "tree bark flakes/plants wither/glaciers melt and slide/ and we watch it on monitors" (from "Corporate Menu"). Once she has her reader thus in thrall, the poet ups the ante in positing a world fueled by despairing travail and the imminence of death: "Can we only be saved in loss?" (from "Epithalamium"). But then it becomes evident that the poet has a different world-view in mind when she juxtaposes such darkness with the idealism of her elegant and touching "Hudson History: Honoring Pete Seeger" in which she infers the redemptive power of hopefulness, of what the world might be, stemming from a new vision. Out from Calaboose is a marvelous, skillful, and evocative work.
–Dr. David B. Austell, Columbia University

With deft craft and convincing imagery KCH deals with the void of change, the world and social disintegration. She says something! Happily, she is far from any current obscurantist mode.
–Roberta Gould, Poet, Translator, Photographer

With rich, metaphorical descriptions, Herceg's honest writing bridges the gap between cultural subconscious and personal experience.
–Zoe Siegel, Lunch Ticket, Antioch University

Karen Corinne Herceg's poems exorcise demons, wring out their vulnerabilities, and fling them into the ether. Her poetry is about survival after much soul searching. Stay tuned for this poet's future work.
–Donna Reis, Poet, Pushcart Prize Nominee

...a favorite for the bold courage of her topics, for how she makes the social and political so personal, often achingly, and for her clear commitment to interpersonal and societal justice...writes with precision, depth and feeling.
–Jonathan Wolfman, Host, Our Salon Radio

The poems are like quilting squares—each stands alone, complete, but hinting at something larger. Each poem reveals just enough without telling too much and without slipping into sentimentality. All quite an achievement.
–Juliana Woodhead, Poetry Editor, The Writing Disorder

Karen Herceg's work is wonderfully macabre, spine-tingling...a joy to read.
–Tess Tabak and e.kirshe, Editors, The Furious Gazelle

...a strong original voice..."Lake Tear of the Clouds" is reminiscent of Walt Whitman and his celebratory lists of the wonders of our world.
–Jean LeBlanc, Executive Editor, Paulinskill Poetry Project

With candor and poise, Karen Corinne Herceg reveals a facet of desiring motherhood...in "Two Olives, Please."
–Maria Scala, Editor-in-Chief, Literary Mama

Herceg's poetry has honesty and a sane, healing quality. As a poet she fulfills one of the most crucial needs of our troubled age: Truth-seeking. There's no pretense in Herceg's approach."
–Robert Milby, Poet & Hudson Valley, NY Poetry Series Host

Karen has a remarkably light touch. Her work, at once hugely imaginative and infinitely relatable, rushes from detail to detail, never losing course or pace. It's only when you near the end of the story that you realise you've been led step-by-step, unknowing, to a sheer drop, and you're not sure if you're ready to go over or not. Surprising in its honesty and sudden beauty... Karen's writing delivers everything you could want.
–Lorrie Hartshorn, Founder & Editor, Halo Literary Magazine, UK

Her work is poignant, biting, tender and pertinent.
–marina mati, Poet & Hudson Valley Howl Radio Host

...so honest and raw.
–Joanna C. Valente, Managing Editor, Luna Luna Magazine

Out from Calaboose *is a terrific and powerful book without a misplaced syllable. It's been awhile since I've read a poetry book cover to cover without a break. But from the first poem the flow of language, executed in detail and imagery, enticed me to read on. The body and mind become victims of gravity; the soul plummets into unknown depth. But then language goes to work, and the poems in* Out from Calaboose *go to work to free the body and mind, to vacate the cell of self and release the emptiness, the creative emptiness the spirit/soul feed on and are nourished by. The poems across the five sections possess energy, a dispassionate passion and generosity in considering the source and sources of imprisonment. They encourage the reader to consider or reconsider his/her own sources of imprisonment by their power and sheer beauty.*
–Richard Martin, Poet, National Endowment for the Arts Fellowship Recipient

NIRALA SERIES

Karen Corinne Herceg

OUT FROM

CALABOOSE

NEW POEMS

With a Foreword by
Roberta Gould

Nirala

Nirala Publications
G.P.O. Box 7004
4637/20, Unit No. 127, Ground Floor
Munish Plaza, Ansari Road
Daryaganj, New Delhi-110002
niralabooks@yahoo.co.in
www.niralapublications.com

First Edition 2017

ISBN 9-788182-500853

Cover Design by Anders Hemlin

Author Photo: Devin Kirschner

Where applicable quotes used with permission of the authors.

Printed at
Chaman Offset Press
New Delhi-2

Preface

The artist's task, then, involves the transformation of the actual to the true.

Louise Glück

It has been over three decades since my first volume of poems, *Inner Sanctions*, was published. At that time I was a young student at Columbia University learning to refine a craft and pursue a passion engendered in me from childhood. In the ensuing years there were many forks in the road. They may have appeared wildly divergent at the time. Now they appear only circular.

It isn't that I didn't write during those many years. But it was a private, mostly introspective time creatively, a subconscious nurturing to a maturity that would bring to fruition my initial, authentic intentions. It is said that some musicians play for the crowd, some for themselves and some to serve the music. When one has tasted so much of the diversity of the world, it either dilutes you or hones your truth. I reached a point where I knew I wanted to serve the "music"—the muse of poetry, and where it took me now would be up to the muse.

And with that realization my work began to evolve again more prolifically and with a deep desire for engagement, not only with the rich literary histories of the world but with an active participation and connection that engendered this work. I share it now with an open heart, a constant yearning for truth, and a humility and gratitude for being able to offer it.

Karen Corinne Herceg
July 2016

Acknowledgements

Grateful acknowledgement is made to the following publications in which several poems in this volume first appeared: "A Thin Season," *Lunch Ticket/Antioch University*, 2016; "A Wake of Frogs,"*The Writing Disorder*, 2015; "After Me, The Poem," *Pyrokinection*, 2016; "Alto Sax," *GFT Press*, 2016; "Betrayer," *The Writing Disorder*, 2015 and *Chronogram*, 2015; "Corporate Menu," *Waymark: Voices of the Valley*, 2015; "Epithalamium For A New Age," *MockingHeart Review*, 2016; "Feline Intensity," *Home Planet News*, 2016; "Hudson History: Honoring Pete Seeger," *The Writing Disorder*, 2015 and *Orange Sullivan Journal*, 2015; "If I Drink Water," *Home Planet News*, 2016; "In My Travels," *Lunch Ticket/Antioch University*, 2016; "In the Silence of the Snow," *Through a Window: Harmony Anthology*, 2011; "Lake Champlain, July," *Badlands Literary Magazine*, 2015 & *Kind of A Hurricane Press/Tranquility Anthology*, 2016; "Loving Hands," *Kind of A Hurricane Press/Shattered Anthology*, 2016; "Out from Calaboose," *Kind of a Hurricane Press/Emergence Anthology*, 2016; "Tableau," *The Writing Disorder*, 2015; "The Glass Vision," *Kind of A Hurricane Press/Reflections Anthology*, 2016; "The Leaving," *The Furious Gazelle*, 2015; "The Natural World," *Badlands Literary Magazine*, 2015; "The Rest," *The Furious Gazelle*, 2015; "Toulon 1971," *Inkwell*, 2012; "Two Olives, Please," *Literary Mama*, 2015 and *Kind of A Hurricane Press/Secrets and Dreams Anthology*, 2016; "Uncollected," *The Avalon Literary Review*, 2016; "Urban Visit," *Home Planet News*, 2016; "Words," *Poetic Licence Magazine*, 2016.

My deepest gratitude to gifted poet Yuyutsu Ram Dass Sharma and Nirala Publications for their faith in me and for publishing my work.

Sincere appreciation to my friend and guide, poet Roberta Gould, for composing the Foreword.

Thank you Linda Gray Sexton for your edits, your kindness and your invaluable advice.

My appreciation to marina mati for reading the following poems on her podcast *Hudson Valley Howl*

at Our Salon Radio, https://archive.org/details/
TheHudsonValleyHowl: "A Wake of Frogs," "Heart,"
"Loving Hands," "The Leaving," "The Natural World,"
"The Rest," "Toulon 1971," and "Two Olives, Please."

I am very grateful to Jonathan Wolfman for his unfailing
support and for reading the following poems on his
radio programs *Passionate Justice* and *Lit Snips* at *oursalon.
ning.com*: "Betrayer," "Corporate Menu," "Hudson
History," "Lake Tear of the Clouds," "Loving Hands,"
"The Leaving," "The Natural World," "The Rest," "Two
Olives, Please," "The Farmer's Market," "Tableau," and
"Uncollected."

My sincere thanks to Robert Milby, the Hudson Valley
Poetry Community, Christi Shannon Kline, Donna
Reis, and Lisa Fleck Dondiego for great support and
suggestions and to all those poets who have gone before
me and those who continue to work so diligently each
day.

My sons, Alexander, Justin and John and granddaughters
Hannah and Sofia Rose: I share with you parts of myself
I hope grow in love and understanding. And Paul: you
share in much of this and I want you to know it.

Love and thanks to Sam Bandes, and to my surrogate
"mom," Mary McKeown.

My love and immeasurable thanks to my life and soul
partner, Stephen McKeown, for his keen eye and wisdom
in reviewing my work.

A Note About the Cover Design:
"Breaking Free" by artist Anders Hemlin, used by
permission from the artist.
From ancient times to the present, the mystery and myth
of the egg is a symbol of birth, rebirth and renewal, yet
a place from which we need to escape in order to claim
the "self." I felt this symbol exemplified so much of my
work.

Thanks to Louise Glück for permission to quote an
excerpt from the essay: "Against Sincerity" in *Proofs &
Theories: Essays on Poetry*, Louise Glück (Ecco, 1994).

Reprinted with kind permission from Harper Collins
Publishers and Carcanet Press Limited, Manchester, UK.

Thanks to Brenda Hillman and The Academy of
American Poets for use of her quote: Brenda Hillman,
"Four Questions for New Academy Chancellor Brenda
Hillman," *American Poets*, Spring-Summer 2016.
Reprinted by permission of the Academy of American
Poets, 75 Maiden Lane, Suite 901, New York, NY
10038. www.poets.org.

Contents

Foreword

In *Out from Calaboose*, Karen Corinne Herceg traces what one might call a karmic trajectory from oppressive relationships in adult life back to a controlling or absent parent whose chiseled stone dates leave "impressions in her flesh." And, after that, to a freeing.

With deft care and pointed imagery we have one who is not a confessional sensationalist but a seeker for meaning: where she was, whoever she may have been, where she is, whatever that may be. In "One Small Stone," she does not know and, with the moving water, arrives. And it is new, this "nascent unlived arrival of myself." In this quest for freedom Herceg sees the lie of limitation. The mother whose "Loving Hands," in the book's key poem, were the start of her struggle will always be there, but the poet achieves real love as she strives for consciousness. In "Alto Sax," with "the curve of your notes, the purse of your lips," she is on her way.

Not limiting herself, we see the poet look beyond the personal to corporate menus of greed and ecological disregard for our earth. Valuing truth, she plumbs deep and gives what we can relate to, not with psychological facileness but with the understanding achieved by staying true to the glimmers she always has had of her essence. We can identify with her personal journey and learn through her art. How refreshing!

Saying less Karen Corinne Herceg says more with pointed fineness. Her eyes "closed like coffin lids" express the prior unconscious state she has emerged from. A time of "hollow auction calls and nothing new" is over. How often a life becomes a "show" when a writer, striving for attention, so common in our populated world, gives unwanted details meant to shock or to perversely repel. This poet, eschewing facile hits, bridges the bad and the ugly as one who, arriving and on a new plain, can breathe freely and share in poems that are an example we will happily profit by. Never trendy, we have here an original in the best sense of the word.

Read on!

Roberta Gould
August 2016

Out From Calaboose

for STEVE
Your light shines on truth and
your honesty teaches me courage

Part One

A Wake of Frogs

All discarded lovers should be given a second chance,
but with somebody else.

--Mae West, (1893-1980)

In My Travels

I can't remember what I left behind...
something in Morocco,
a one-day trip on a ferry with goats
around the rock of Gibraltar,
women swathed in black sheets
oblivious to the heat,
their disallowed energy
herding chickens on the weather worn deck,
coal fired eyes avoiding mine.
I am a woman too,
have herded children, objects and desires.

On this other continent
sweat woven rugs are hawked to me,
okra and moss colored herbal tinctures
hold promises to cure what I cannot;
a swell of odors wafts through
narrow, primeval alleyways,
huddles of figures in stone hollows
bake barbaric bread on stone pallets
extended to me by nomadic hands,
primary sustenance
like old communion
dry and stiff on my tongue.
A curved backed Bedouin
shines a seller's smile
a toothless mouth and beggar's hand
offering objects I can take home
to narrate my journey.

Back at the hotel
the coast of Spain is blurred
through a rain embossed window,
tears streaking

for the sweater I left behind
in the store of the ruby frocked merchant,
fez tassel swirling among his wares.
And all the spoils and discount deals
cannot replace the history of my sweater
sitting alone an ancient culture away,
never to come home again.

Shadow Dance

Face down
toward the earth
legs held tightly
arms spread wide
you cover me
like a crucifix
impaled on the strength
of your compulsion.
We puzzle lock into
one form
our outline reflected
wall shadows
puppets of the sun
in another day's burst
dark and light converging
force and release
gain and loss
balancing
blending
as the parts
grow into whole
separate
blanched into day

The Glass Vision

You wanted to build,
build a structure,
a monument to your worth,
of your worthiness to me
the prize you won,
but could not hold.
You carried slabs of wood,
pouches of nails;
studied blueprints,
veins stretching
across the paper
into a vision of your world.
That house:
too grand to hold
the comfort of a family,
too bold to assimilate us
into the patterns of the land,
the community,
setting us apart from neighbors
and one another.
How many birds did we lose
cascading into walls of windows
that reflected sun-speckled light
that deceived them
into thinking a horizon was there
when only death awaited,
hard hit endings,
carcasses lined along the entrance
to a dream
too large to last,
our bodies lost within cavernous rooms,
windows all around, skylights, glass
and endless vistas,
specks beyond distance
expansive to the point of gone.

A Wake of Frogs

An early April day, arms full of grocery bags,
frost in the air not yet done,
I walked toward the house, stopped,
stunned by the sudden sight,
their gleaming bodies
laid out across rocks rimming the fountain
like civil war soldiers
waiting to be recognized and buried.
The porch where I sat evenings
watching the small waterfall
leech through rocks
frothing into a pool rimmed with tiger lilies
was far from soothing now.
How to know the autumn before
ice would seal a wet tomb
before those innocents could escape?
A city girl, I couldn't warn them
or know of nature's ways.

Bags fallen at my feet, I spotted him
through our picture window
sitting casually, *New York Times* in hand.
How he loved the crossword puzzle,
its setup of boxes, the clean neat lines,
the completion of tiny words,
the supposition of victory.
This was complete, too:
death at the end of long years,
memories frozen over with no future
laid out to view.
He thought those frogs were a warning
but they were only seeking a proper burial,
an affirmation
of what was long deceased.

Valentine: 2-14-88

You see there is no denying
what I feel for you my love,
but my eyes close
against the light,
little coffin lids
closing to the surety
of the secret.
I fear you'll carve me
like a main course,
make a toast
and drink my blood
thickened by the fire of you.
My great swollen heart
sits high in the chest,
feels the start of vivisection,
pumps against the prick
of the point
at the end of
your blade
where it will be consumed.
Yet I can't move.
Pieces of my body,
host to you,
cling to your pores,
absorb me.
And if you don't finish the job,
my love,
I will.

The Poem Survives the Romance

I was so angry
at the chicken hawk
blatant branched perching
above me
with overt desire
erect for prey
no decency
to hide the wish
for triumph
a clawing conqueror
patient in its unhidden
revealed pulse
quickening upon
the object
that allows its surrender

Epithalamium for a New Age

Who is making the sacrifice?
Who is giving something away...taking
something?
Bloodletting...the spot they hung out on the
purest white sheet
for the world to acknowledge;
old wives secretly glad to admit another
member
to their world of relinquishment,
the loss of giving
in an act we call sacred.
Can we only be saved in loss?
Only sanctioned in ritual?

It is not marriage itself
but all that we have changed
to implicate it
into our helpless legalities,
desperate desires,
Cinderella carriages
ballroom princes
majestic mcmansions
and progeny like products
poised on the edge
at the end
of elaborate profitable receptions.

The slow trot begins
up ceremonial aisles,
trailing trains and mystic veils
unleashing surrender
and unrestrained expectations
into the heritage of ownership,
a bondage

fearful of its own detention,
dredging us through
the approbation of attendants, guests
who willingly welcome you to their world
of shared disillusions
and the others, still waiting to yoke
themselves,
stare with the anticipation of the innocent.

Rather you strip me down
and yoke me stark
pare and parse the lace
the sugar that hides the taste
of me
honesty in your need
to own my love.

Feline Intensity

She regards him
with a feline intensity
the pierce of question
disguised as bravado
fake it 'till you make it
says the swish of the tail
the come hither
bait and switch love trap
that knows you want it
so she gives it
hoarding triumph
like a flag
raised
while gazing in the moist aftermath
her eyes following sky-framed rooftops
that keep reaching.

Cats never look hurt:
just indignant.

If I Drink Water

If I drink water
I expect no flavor;
but you are selling me tea,
coffee, juiced up beverages
you swear I can taste
off the drip of you.
My tongue,
much too practiced
notices,
and my spirit,
much too experienced,
wants
the zest it craves
and will return to
water
when you leave
and pure nourishment
begins.

When It Ended

It is all firmly rooted
in a sea of self-imposed despair
birds cackling at me in the morning
although others say they are singing
squirrels scamper but they are only afraid
running always running
my theories of what you will say
lost in the footsteps of chasing you
only cause more confusion
words stampede out of my mouth
like hollow auction calls
you smile slyly like you know
but shake your head sadly
at my misquotes aimed
to please you along with
a good pot roast
but they will all be excreted
turned into utterings of leftovers
used before and recycled
only nothing was new or invented
and you noticed

Part Two

In the Silence of the Snow

Poetry, even when apparently most fantastic,
is always a revolt against artifice, a revolt,
in a sense, against actuality.
--James Joyce, (1882-1941)

Sprung

Walk with me
against the chill
and I'll recite
the opening stanzas
from *The Canterbury Tales*
springing from the envelope
of my Ivy League embossed memory.
I'll enchant you
with useless but stunning
rhymes and clever rhythms
and airborne promises
of natural order
and romance.
None of it will
further your career
or keep you warm
or safe from scrutiny.
It will repeat you
into the future
of the already by-gone
living in indulgent recreation
each time April
rings back again.

April Note

I trace the veins
of each leaf opening
along the journey
of frozen memories
in a changing tableau
where once I stretched out
unable to rise
like a frost-bitten animal
in the snow.
And now I sit
upright, looking outward,
all points of me
coming together
as in a Seurat,
on the extended
green-fringed limb
of expectation.
An open hand.

Summer Excuses

I never liked the noonday sun,
its growling intensity,
the way I mishandle its discomfort,
its brazen eye
conspicuously unsympathetic
to my exposure,
the aroma of tar
released from smoldering pavements,
the need to push through the air
thick and smoky with heat,
sweat bubbling to the surface
of my pores,
the lethargy of days passing,
inertia of bodies,
the effort of time to move forward,
the propulsion required for accomplishment,
regrets for missed deadlines,
the agony of what will not prevail.
I long for a restorative breeze
to lift the horizon,
to slant in
seize the stagnant air,
to admonish me
for the insult
of my impatience
for what I cannot tolerate
in a seasonal world.

Autumn Waits

The day screams colder
presuming bare
desperate winter trees.
Leaves bleed out colors,
sap freezing in their veins,
skies running bleak.
I build fires
against a frigid
unforgiving horizon,
fabricating warmer hope,
when climate will not mirror
the measure of my soul,
dictate rhythms of desires,
the direction of spirit.
When melting or igniting
will not be issues
within the waiting.

Winter's Beginning

That hard frost
hits the bone
etches its way
through the spiraling bare branches
of winter.
I see the puzzle of a sky
between skeletal fingers
and its stark patches
bore into me
like a hopeless romance.
I cook with homely herbs
on a burgeoning fire
and imagine you.
I would like to feed you
this food,
nourish the world's sparse horizon,
warm you
as I can only do now
with spring notes
hidden in unborn images.
There could be new life
in me
if we could find our way,
and in the joining
we would know no seasons.

In the Silence of the Snow

The pressure of snowfall
eases sound from the air
shifting noise
to the edges of earth.
Cries soften
shouts fade to whispers
dissipating into
layers of cold fog
rising off the powdered fields
of serenity.
In that endless white horizon
peace is a verb
zero is a virtue
and action is spared comment
envisioning oneness
with every cell and nuance
in the silence of the snow.

Alto Sax

I smoke through the air
on the curve of your notes
at the purse of your lips
your horn the instrument
of my pleasure

only the note is pure
we are suspect
so I ride the melody to forgiveness
of myself
for hearing such music

I am prepared to lose my sight
but not the sound of having you
nor the history
nor the collection of moments
nor the time spent listening

nor the wonder
if it can be retrieved
like an item lost
I only know
the song is now

Toulon 1971

Miguel Amor,
I see you older now,
a family man,
the lawyer you had said you would become,
defending criminals in Madrid,
a place where I have never been, where I
imagine a russet sunset
reflecting off wine colored brick houses
as you walk home in the evening.
When I think of Spain
it is black and red:
The bull and the teaser
inviting one another.

Miguel Amor,
I never wanted to become a woman
in young America,
in borrowed cars of unsuspecting fathers,
in a place so close to home.
It's like a mission, you see,
where a stranger is welcome and fed,
but you never really get to know him.
Do you remember:

There was no wind in Toulon in August.
The road was long from the stone beach
and Mediterranean blue
to the motel of modest rooms
each with lights like votive candles,
an oasis where no one really lives,
a stopping point
where days are long
like the tanned, moist limbs
of languishing nudes.

In the white glare of an afternoon
I watched you stroll up the dirt road
while, straw hat in hand, I fanned the heavy air,
the grass yellow and dry cracking like wheat
between my toes, and
we walked on the beach at dusk,
the sand becoming dark and musty,
breath, dust and salt air drifting together.
I felt you like a sacrifice,
a frail membrane struggling
on the mild sea air.

Miguel Amor,
at twenty you were a man,
or so it seemed to me,
walking back down the road,
waving promises I did not want you to keep.
And that letter you sent
was really a subtle consolation,
unnecessary: the crime as hot,
as innocent
as feeling.

Gravity

You will come to me.
I stare you down,
practice on your image
retained securely
behind my patch of an eye.
You circle in my private spaces,
a planet in orbit
drawn into a magnetic field.
Our masks lock,
clink loudly.
We tear at our faces
with numb fingers,
our flesh melts like a flake.
Finally reduced by our own image
we fold into one another.
Time chimes clocks
as if it were a gift;
all of space: a concept in a text.
You have come to me.

Tableau

The world
scaled for living
presses against a zero-degree sky,
the day's beginning light
opening like a book.
The morning so frozen
will not allow the gibbous moon
to retire,
hovering over still-waiting lamplights,
poor imitations,
all their nightly duty done.
And I: supine across the linens
before this scene
as in a Rousseau tableau,
lying like a cut-out
in my own jungle,
each part outlined clearly
like the white snow-capped roofs
against the icy blue horizon.
And still
I think that you will edge me off the canvas
and paste me to the landscape
where you live.

Part Three

A Thin Season

*He who does not bellow the truth when he knows
the truth makes himself the accomplice of liars and forgers.*
--Charles Péguy, (1873-1914)

Betrayer

The truth is
this is a fearful place,
constant trembling
flanked with platitudes,
with magical thinking,
failure drowning in cocktails,
lust laughing in a sophomoric comedy
as smoke curls
through the affluent air.
There's a lot of leftover
hippie love
and broken philosophies.
We assent to camouflage,
a whimsical toast,
a sea of well wishing,
the rejuvenation of a spa weekend.
Before the dusk of empty bottles,
pill prompted memories,
a closing door,
we consider praying again,
measures of redemption
kicking us back onto the cross,
always just shy of resurrection.

Corporate Menu

Don't we love the raw beauty
of the starkly indigent,
the thought of their rough brown hands,
hands of earth we swear to revere
handing us our designer coffee,
hand picked beans from field to table;
vegetables harvested under the sun's pierce
from nurturing rays to fluorescent lit aisles,
petroleum plastic packaged
for the convenience of our impatient lives,
a slow sneak of toxic death,
engineered crops
clothed in the garb of healthy nourishment.
Can't you see the peasant,
the juxtaposition
of his coca cola embossed tee shirt
with his indigo, lizard green, plum,
poppy colored poncho
woven from his own hands
from an animal he raised
in a place we will never know.
The cool current of unpolluted streams
is on a time clock,
tree bark flakes
plants wither
glaciers melt and slide
and we watch it on monitors
all of it a click away
heedless that empty shelves
will stare us down
stripped harshly by our own greed.

A Thin Season

*For a young man beheaded for listening to Western pop tunes
in his father's grocery store.*

It is a thin season
culling the air of blue breath
choked sudden as a sword
at the throat of a young infidel
the forbidden pop tune of his innocence
still playing in the annals
of his thoughts
kneeling, repetitive, insistent
as the accusations of the faithful
who behead him
on an afternoon like any other
clouds rising
in a decimation of distance
between the neck and heaven.
Isis goddess of love, the moon,
magic and fertility,
a healing sister of deities
daughter of earth and sky,
twists in a massacre
of celestial delusions
bearing the severed body
back to the arms that bore him,
the one who will hear music
no more.

Hudson History

Honoring Pete Seeger

We've assumed you
beyond your natural shifts and turns,
morphing historical perspective,
birthing ourselves into your river grace,
iron and metal bridged
across your girth,
wave against will.
Adaptable in a marketable world,
your iconic flow
no exception,
your pristine nature filled
with natives and intruders,
the lush natural and
the burden of the built,
from ambitious towers
to towering trees
to the tread of silence
near old wilderness.
You begin at the north,
the top,
and push your power south,
carrying all,
delivering in a democracy of spirit,
challenged, fierce then passive,
history glinting off your journeys,
truth remaining in your depths,
powering through the harbor,
your own story
obscured by ours.

Lake Tear of the Clouds

Highest pond of empire state,
     Lake Tear of the Clouds wellsprings
          the Hudson River matriarch,
its three hundred and fifteen mile journey
     escaping from the heart into the harbor,
          a mirror of explorers' reflections
through trails of Adirondack royalty,
     glacial sculpted, bracing the land
          where a great flow of history begins.

But your artery bleeds too:
     cries of acid rain,
          the bloodletting of commerce,
voyagers, revolutionaries, patriots, soldiers,
     mercenaries, bootleggers, escaped prisoners
          slaves, commuters.
Old Albany Post Road
     conceded horse, stagecoach, car
          furrowing the stretch of transport

alongside Great Mohegan,
     North River, Great River,
          your piers and byways
pierced by ambitious trade,
     crossed by pioneers,
          spliced with tunnels,
bridges dissecting your breadth
     for posterity
          and prosperity.

The ships, the cargo, the populated
     parse themselves along your banks
          waning northward against the current,

becoming sparser,
>   where one begins recovery of the path,
>   the wayfarer, the solitary,
returning to the origin
>   where opal clouds, hovering witnesses,
>   await salvation,
weeping another rupture,
>   vaporizing into promise
>   for Lake Tear of the Clouds.

The Farmer's Market

I fear leaving home
in a news driven world.
Where is the hope?
Buried deeply in all the guns,
beheadings, crucifixions?

My own hope is in greens and fruits,
a farmer's market,
stalls standing fierce against open air,
tethered to grassy firmament.
I count on it wet or dry,
cool or hot,
to nourish me, inside and out,
faithful, constant.
But I worry I make hope too easy,
that it will deceive me.

Rose puts produce in my earth saving bags,
always there with undemanding solace
as she sorts, packs, smiles,
unaware she is giving me hope.

Home, safe behind doors,
I sort through food pushed up
through black dirt
only hours earlier,
knowing no danger yet.
I prune their limbs
and nail them to a cutting board,
snip and deny their roots,
separate them from their stems.
And then I consume them
before they can censor themselves,
filling a space I call fear.

The Natural World

I am astonished
at what I do not see
in the world,
what lies microscopically
below the surface
of a pedestrian eye.
What atoms are rearranging themselves,
what nascent cells plot their appearance
into the visual world,
where hummingbirds might be in December,
how things do not transgress, fall apart
more than they do.
We see all with the same eyes,
buying a peach is the same as buying
a work of art.
We transfer hate and love
as commodities,
no singular discrimination,
an equal opportunity
employer of banality.
We draw objects into
our own spheres
dilute them, redefine them,
mute them,
molding them
to our own worlds,
objects that will laugh when they outlive us.
How can we begin to see
until we release impressions
from the skewed centrifuges

of our personal days.
I think how much at peace
every other life remains
in a natural world
they know is hostile,
the one we make aberrant
thinking we can tame it.

Changing of the Guard

Mangy, resigned you sit
in the needle pins of rain
at my door,
fur matted, eyes milky.
I have no way of knowing
what you see
but you hear,
your chewed ears perking at all sounds,
signals to all things
who dwell outdoors
subject to the imposition
of a harsh physical earth.
You were once the supreme commander
of territory, alpha male
protecting your turf.
But there's always another challenge
around the corner
lurking like a clock with a placid face
but still, the ticking.
A tiger striped force of feral ferocity
has usurped your kingdom,
decimated your space,
subjugated your surfs.
No longer leading the pack
you wait now
eating after the others
like the elder in the corner, an afterthought.
You have not lost sustenance
but there's a fissure
in your spirit, a soul seepage,

a black hole collapsing on itself
that food cannot feed,
that causes your stride to slip
and your pride to weaken
while an errant new star burns
its twinkle like a wink
that diminishes you
where your worth is buried.

Urban Visit

In the city
trees are parentheses
urban partitions
their branches
connectors to broken air
a million bodies
scattered together
an upheaval of intentions
buildings the height of monsters
in old Japanese movies
blotting sky
scraps of natural light
dropping into florescent glare
Times Square neon frenzy
blinding minds
wandering through it
imagining purpose
retinal detachment
the flowering iris
hiding its bouquet
glances of deception
fertilizing our wounds

Nano Thought

Higgs is the particle that gives other particles their mass,
making it both centrally important and seemingly magical.
We tend to think of mass as an intrinsic property of all things,
yet physicists believe that without the Higgs boson, mass
fundamentally doesn't exist. A boson is a so-called "force
carrier" for the Higgs field. It is known as the God Particle.

No matter how many times
I read the non-technical
descriptions of quantum physics,
matter, space,
the Higgs boson
tiny particles behaving with
more symmetry than people ever could,
it's all still random
and cannot mimic
the clear true patterns
of a universe
observing us with indulgence;
we in our asymmetrical ambitions,
crossed purposes,
defying one another,
redefining ourselves
against the order of the cosmos.
What if evil is not evil
just negative consequences
of the fearful mind,
the reasonable mind
that suffers in its lack
of the mystical.

Part Four

Loving Hands

*If I feel physically as if the top of my head were taken off,
I know that it's poetry.*
--Emily Dickinson, (1830-1886)

Maternal Elegy

The way the morning light
pardons the night,
that's the absolution I seek,
birthing myself
through a placenta of debts,
cutting the cord
where you dragged me
through the mire
of your own sins;
a maternal bloodbath,
the unendurable obligation
of love,
my eyes sewn shut
by your needle fingers
your voice
consuming my breath,
twenty, forty, sixty years
pressed into the corners
of a lifetime,
nothing to reclaim,
from dry, splintered bones
my freedom hell-bent granted
unpunctual
like
a posthumous degree.

The Leaving

It's not the leaving,
it's the getting out,
mommy whispered
through glazed eyes
rheumy with loss.
The unavoidable last breath,
the chest heaving,
a final rise against time
that will soon cease in one body.
The hiss of oxygen,
a tank of lungs,
machines replacing body parts
that have surrendered
long before spirit.
It all murmurs on.
It's the price for becoming timeless,
to enter a forever place
that we tricked ourselves
into thinking a body might be.

The Rest

My parents rest in drawers of steel,
within shiny, cushioned boxes
behind walls of stone.
Slid in like bakers' trays,
but they will not rise,
will not resurrect,
and it's for the best.
I couldn't withstand
a re-birth,
not for any of us.
We had our chance.
I'll go it alone now,
resting my head against
the cool marble,
the inscription of their names,
the chiseled dates
making impressions on my flesh.

The Search

Sunlight splices through grass,
spots of time
through a congestion of thought
disrupting my search for constancy,
a steady reassuring
pulse of order
I attempt to extract
from a faltering spirit.
How did I become
a ghost,
an apparition to those
I craved would see me,
the truthful lingering me,
the me whose shadow
now addresses itself
in a tender voice
it calls home.

Two Olives, Please

Mommy takes a long swig of cocktail,
always a chance for blurt,
a revelation somehow
of something we never wanted.
Did you know,
and so it begins.
There's another sister somewhere,
on another shore,
another one of you.
Wide-eyed, my sister and I
pause
as she orders another martini.
Two olives, please.

This third remains unknown.
It was the war and Daddy was lonely,
she sighs and sips,
didn't know the possibility of us,
couldn't make it right on foreign shores.
He was blinded by Mommy's shiny allure,
undefined promises
beckoning him homeward.
So the baby disappeared
decades gone
into distant geography.
She shows up now,
amid swish and clink
at this luncheon of sly glances
and gaping mouths,
watching us silently
from another womb.

Uncollected

I awake to the immeasurable sadness
of loss,
not for whatever was
but what was not,
the dream of possibilities and lost connections,
the incurable pain of memories
that never existed.
Mama
I thought you loved me
and would care for your own flesh,
but you wrung out of me
what you could not get
from your absent father,
philandering german boy
whose pockets you searched as a child
for pennies, for food he drank away.
And you took him in years later
big, groaning and diabetic
handing over his monthly check
proudly
as if he thought that could feed you now,
could take back the cold water flats,
the hunger for more than food.
And you nourished him in your home
with heat and comfort,
still he only grunted
and moved his great paw
roughly across your head,
still no words, no request for forgiveness
just you leaning over his dying face,
your tears begging,
his eyes vacant staring beyond yours
as he hissed the lament of growing old,
of leaving food and drink and women,

but no mention of you.
And when I leaned over your hospice bed
looked at you with tears for the last time
you only saw through me
into the fog
of what you think you lost,
but no mention of me.

Excuses of the Heart

The brain fills pockets of loss
collated by a shifting memory
that wants what it wants and not what it saw.
Terror from my mother's fears was less frightening
than the resigned abdicating eyes of my father
although it appeared to be different on the surface
where we live most days blinking against thoughts
that reveal something true
against the excuses of the heart.
No one can see us if we shun our shadows, shaded
from the self. It's my shadow that shows you who I am.
And you will think that you miss me after I leave,
that you see me around a corner, in a theatre,
in someone wearing the same hat I wore.
But you never saw me, so
I could be anyone.

Undone

My lover understands
afraid
pulls thorns from my
heart
removes the noose
coveting my throat
tells me it's fine
to be five again
to look up
see the monsters
how they smiled
while handling me
maneuvered into lost places
brutally pushed out
into a placenta of expectation
navigating a fog
yoking me
daring to look back
Lot's wife smiling
not disintegrating
cutting the cord

Loving Hands

Kneeling in opposite corners
facing pale yellow walls
spines straight as rulers
with impressions from loving hands,
my sister and I learned early
about a queen who must be obeyed,
about disorderly conduct,
an education of belt welts
for transgressions only children can commit,
guilty for disturbing
Mommy's perfect world,
interrupting phone calls,
scattering dirt,
ruffling the sheer, ironed curtains.

Lists of duties
created by loving hands
made checkmarks in our minds,
leaving nothing to chance
in the heavy finality of demands.
I dusted and polished
until shine clashed with brightness
watching with escalating horror
as dust particles cascaded in
on sheaths of bold sunlight
streaking my hopes for salvation.
I scrubbed and scoured
with the diligence of rescue,
while living behind stone works,
a factory churning and forging tombstones,
the daily pounding and polishing,
mimicking my efforts
sawing through stone
screeching in my ears

as I scrambled to stave
the many ways to perish.

Doing subverted being
destroying us faster than inevitability.
I married the order in order to be safe
but my sister divorced its harsh importance
screaming *look at me.*
Each night loving hands scrubbed me,
an invasion admonishing the dirt
I could no longer see.
I waited in bed, under cover,
for those loving hands
showing me what I should not know
in the dark where I could not see.
Daddy, a silent witness,
fed pills to his failing organs
rowing his boat steadily
while whispering to me
that life is but a dream
before disappearing quietly.
Years later my sister said,
she looks at you like a lover
and she hates me for it.
She would rather have been chosen
than ignored by loving hands,
the chasm widening between us
until we spoke no more,
the bruises in our minds raw
and spreading like thick, red welts.

Mommy organized her departure
calling my ear close to her lips
hissing that now I could be free,
released from loving hands.
But I could not let the dust settle
glass streak, dishes dry on their own,

my sons growing neat and clean in her wake,
learning early that clothes are washed
before hugs are earned.

I find myself always in lessening days,
reflections startling
as time moves me further toward recognition.
My eyes shift
from the stare in the mirror,
the glare that resembles mine,
the hands I study, holding them up wondering
in front of my squinting eyes,
if they combat the inheritance,
the long lines of cut stone
insisting we had existed,
engraved with the legacy
of loving hands.

But I am my own jihad,
refusing to be sabotaged,
looking out into a globe of parts
I do not know,
the nascent, unlived arrival of myself
defying the gravity of stone,
recovering cell by cell,
a sculptor's excavation.
Until I begin to see the outline
the reaching to embrace,
loving hands that now hold me
in the arms of my own soul.

Part Five

Out from Calaboose

For small creatures such as we the vastness is bearable only
through love.
--Carl Sagan, (1934-1996)

Alternatives

Seeing the light in another window,
a hope for which I want no responsibility,
allows permission to imagine
all the lives I could have had
had I not had this one:
the greener grass,
the thoughtful, caring parent,
a lineage of Mayflower generations
instead of a fragmented, immigrant-infused
history of misfits and losses.
But I am only imagining,
imbuing strangers with untenable attributes.
One day none of them will be present,
will speak to me without words again
stripped of mundane fever and pain,
and the physical remnants
of what we believed ourselves to be,
believed we were forgiven.
Vaults of hurt and memory
bury us long before gravity binds us
to a shifting earth,
a legacy less than the one hoped for.

One Small Stone

The odd thing about erosion
is what it does not take away.
You skip the stone,
water rippling in rhythmic disturbance,
diverting the stream
in a serpentine trail
switching direction
imperceptibly,
a shutter of moments
before it sinks.
Silently it pushes a new course
in unseen fathoms
where you do not want to go.
But your eyes strain down its route,
seeking the subtlety of immersion,
startled at how it shifted,
bound you to its will,
took you along to its depths.
Even your reflection changes
as you gaze downward
into its liquid question:
how you got to another point,
to another shore,
alone
without a raft,
wondering.

Out From Calaboose

(Calaboose: Jail; especially a local one)

The variety of prisons
boggles choice,
disturbs the brain's logic,
determination wide
to imagine escape.
It begins with
one clean brick,
hurled against rage,
of what we will not release,
morphs into fade
under the mortar of hardship
we draw to us.
False impressions,
pride and blame.
And revenge,
that pitiful gallows mask.
Ropes tighten or loosen
as we walk through
memory-splattered gardens
to ancient slatted doors,
grilled iron
and locked rooms
that once we ran toward
so greedily.

Home In You

I've grown so distant
from the plates, the armchair,
the table,
from a still life of functions
and daily considerations.
A chasm filled with years
and unfinished memories
hangs in the spaces
of our present distance
an intangible throbbing ache.
If I could thrust my hands outward
ripping through embryonic clay
I would sculpt the lives
we did not have
to pull you through the places
we were not
until we reached a place
we could be
whole and new.
Saved by me.
Home in you.

The Intruder

rest inside sullen shadow
as if earth did not birth new each morning
like the first time
in a Bible story
the one we all want to believe
as if immersion
a baptism
could strain the dark from the light
as if words could make coherency
and angels hovered above us
just waiting for some sign of recognition
acceptance
and belief without seeing
dueling and dying the big noises
will we still be heard if we whisper
seen if we hide
here in our sleep
be distained if we whimper
applauded if we hang on and
deny our dreams
as if they were not reality

Lake Champlain, July

I float in a view
of sculpted distant peaks
mountains of New York height
across the Lake of
great Champlain,
a humid free July evening
before fireflies are detected.
Trees that pine across the ripples
of skyline
breathe the smooth, clear air
and haunt the hills that hold them.
The horizon shifts with the mind
but the water shifts with the heart
forging a clear outline
only thought can fog.
Distortion is the work of doubt,
clarity the simple vision of imperfection
leaving space for volume.
If I move from consciousness
I, too, can pine and water shift,
a shape switch spirit
from head to soul.

Words

The word makes a liar
when it leaves the lip, the pen;
we put too much confidence in the eyes,
the ears, the mouth.
Flesh and bone-in
I prefer the authenticity of the disturbed
whose fears are better focused,
a knife-sliced reality.
We cut ourselves
to feel the pain
a heart cannot hold.
Can we not grant ourselves the grace
to remain defenseless,
become a footnote,
the greater honesty in the small print,
losing artificial assumptions.
And what will words become at my hand
that they have not been before.

After Me, The Poem

I stand beneath it,
the moon too many people
have written about,
that expectant orb
poised for answers.
I'm sure it's had enough of us
and just shines for itself
watching us backslap
our latest error
mistaken for achievement,
the supposition of inspiration.

Will anything stave off this thing
called salvation--
how if we pine and ponder enough
somehow we will deserve explanations
for all the unexplained places
bookmarked in our minds
so we don't forget to go back
revisit them--
as if giving ourselves more time
will provide solutions,
guidance.

I stare up at the dark remnant
of the hole where that moon sat
only moments before,
now hidden,
its thin remaining cartoon outline
a sketchy dubious reflection
of another light,
borrowed brightness,
deceptively skirting across horizons
flirting with our serious

studies of its barren landscape,
our man in the moon wishes,
its vanishing act each morning
leaving us stark-eyed
staring at harsher glare
lighting our stage,
in the daylight of dreams
waiting to perform
more questions we will ask
after living another day.

And this poem
will still teach
long after I lose
the will for instruction.

Nirala Series
A Series of Contemporary Writing

All Vows
New &   Selected Poems
David B. Austell
ISBN 9-788182-500822 pp.194 2016 Paper Demy

Fulcrum
Selected Poems
Irene O' Garden
ISBN 9-788182-500860 pp.88 2017 Paper Demy

Out from Calaboose
New Poems
Karen Corinne Herceg
ISBN 9-788182-500853 pp.91 2017 Paper Demy

The Tin Man
David B. Austell
ISBN 9-788182-500792 2017 pp.320 Hard Demy

A Blizzard in My Bones
New York Poems
Yuyutsu Sharma
ISBN 81-8250-070-2 2016 pp.134 Paper

Inside the Shell of the Tortoise
Poems written in India and Nepal
A Spanish English Edition
Veronica Aranda
Translated by **Claudia Routon** *with* **Yuyutsu Sharma**
ISBN 9-788182-500686 2016 pp.56 Hard

Your Kiss is a River
Poems of Love, Food and Life
Carolyn Wells
ISBN 9-788182-500532 2016 pp.56 Hard

Poemas de los Himalayas
A Spanish/English edition
Yuyutsu Sharma
Translated by Veronica Aranda
ISBN 81-8250-070-2 2015 pp.134 Paper
Collaboration with **Juan de Mairena y de libros,**
Cordoba, Spain

TEN: The New Indian Poets
Selected and Edited by
Jayanta Mahapatra & Yuyutsu Sharma
ISBN 9-788182-500341 2012 pp.134 Hard

Everest Failures
Twenty Five Short Poems
Yuyutsu Sharma
ISBN 9-788182-500464 2012   Hard pp.48

Prisoner of an ipad
Arun Budhathoki
ISBN 9-788182-500570 2014   Paper pp.64

Milarepa's Bones, Helambu
33 New Poems
Yuyutsu RD Sharma
ISBN 9-788182-500327 2012   Hard pp.64

Garuda
& Other Astral Poems
David B. Austell
ISBN 9-788182-500389 2012   Hard pp.72

Annapurna Poems
Poems New and Selected
Yuyutsu RD Sharma
ISBN 9-788182-500471 2014 Hard pp.150

Inside Out, Upside Down,
& Round and Round
Poems Selected & New
John J. Trause
ISBN 9-788182-500495 2012   Paper pp.83

Safa Tempo
Poems Selected and New
Bhuwan Thapaliya
ISBN 9-788182-500365 2011   Paper pp.50

All the way from Kathmandu
Selected Jazz Poems
John Clarke
ISBN 9-788182-500426 2012   Paper pp.82

No Child More Perfect
& Other Poems
Christi Shannon Kline
ISBN 9-788182-500396 2012   Paper pp.82

Things Missed in Exile
New Poems
E. Avi Frishman
ISBN 9-788182-500556 2012 Paper pp. 49

Journey Though India and Nepal
Poems/Pictures
Robert Scotto & Lu Wu
ISBN 9-788182-500457 2012   Hard pp.84

Incident on the Orient
Poems by
George Wallace
ISBN 9-788182-500440 2012   Paper pp. 76

Lizard Licking, Donegal *& Other Poems*
Diane Hamilton
ISBN 9-788182-500334 2011 Paper pp 82

The Price of Heaven
Travel Stories from India and Nepal
Evald Flisar
*Translated from Slovene by the **Author & Alan McConnell-Duff***
ISBN 9-788182-500556 2009 Paper pp.140

Baghdad, February 1991
&Other Poems
Ronny Someck
Translated into Nepali by **Yuyutsu RD Sharma**
ISBN 81-8250- 018-4 2009 Hard pp.200

After Tagore
Poems Inspired by **Rabindranath Tagore**
David Ray
ISBN 81-8250-007-9 2007 Hard pp. 115

Hunger of Our Huddled Huts
& Other Poems
Yuyutsu R.D.
ISBN 81-85693-80-3 2007 pp.65

Kathmandu
Poems Selected and New (An English/Nepali Bilingual Edition)
Cathal O Searcaigh
Translated from the Gaelic by **Seamus Heaney,**
John Montague and others
Translated into the Nepali by **Yuyutsu R.D. Sharma**
ISBN 81-8250-006-0 2006 Hard pp. 105

The Lake Fewa & a Horse
Poems New
Yuyutsu R.D. Sharma
ISBN 81-85693-34-X 2005 Paper pp. 108

Muna Madan
A Play in the Jhyaure Folk Tradition
Laxmi P. Devkota
Translated from the Nepali by **Anand P. Shrestha**
ISBN 81-85693-94-3 2000 pp.65

Fever (Short Stories)
Sita Pandey
Translated from the Nepali
ISBN 81-85693-93-5 2001 Paper pp.96

Says Meera
An Anthology of Devotional Songs of Meera,
India's Greatest Woman Poet
Translated from the Hindi by **Vijay Munshi**
ISBN 81-85693-96-X 2001 Paper pp.76

Some Female Yeti & other Poems
Yuyutsu R.D.
ISBN 81-8250-010-9 2007 pp.68

In the City of Partridges (Poems)
Jagdish Chatturvedi
ISBN 81-85693-99-4 2004 Paper pp.90

Roaring Recitals: Five Nepali Poets
Gopal Prasad Rimal, Bhupi Sherchan, Shailendra & Others
Translated from the Nepali by
Yuyutsu R.D. Sharma
ISBN 81-85693-95-1 1999 Hard pp.99

Sheet of Snow
An Anthology of Stories from the Himalayas
Translated from the Nepali by **Nagendra Sharma**
ISBN 81-85693-61-7 1997 paper pp.125

Dispossessed Nests: The 1984 Poems
Jayanta Mahapatra
ISBN 81-85693-74-9 1986 pp.69 Paper